Best wishes,
Tom Selleck

Giving Love *a* Memory

CREATING TRADITIONS YOUR FAMILY WILL CHERISH

HARVEST
HOUSE
PUBLISHERS

Eugene, Oregon 97402

Giving Love a Memory

Copyright © 1997 by Linda Lee and Ruthann Winans
Published by Harvest House Publishers
Eugene, Oregon 97402

Library of Congress Cataloging-in-Publication Data
Winans, Ruthann
    Giving love a memory / Ruthann Winans and Linda Lee.
        p. cm.
    ISBN 1-56507-659-1 (hardcover)
    1. Family—Religious life. 2. Christian life. I. Lee, Linda, 1958-   . II. Title
    BV4526.2.W56 1997
    249—dc21   97-9436
                                                   CIP

Cover image: Li'l Dipper © 1992 S. Thomas Sierak and Wild Wings, Inc., Lake City, MN

Unless otherwise noted, all works of art reproduced in this book are copyrighted by S. Thomas Sierak and may not be copied or reproduced without the artist's permission. For information regarding prints featured in this book, please contact:

    S. Thomas Sierak Fine Art
    192 Nashua Road
    Dracut, MA 01826
    (508) 957-1391

Design and production by Left Coast Design, Portland, Oregon

Permissions and acknowledgments: The "Rhubarb Pie Story" in the prolog is retold by Linda Lee; originally published in *Values from the Heartland* by Bettie B. Youngs (Deerfield Beach, FL: Health Communications, Inc. 1995). "Sweet Dreams Cookies" recipe from Frances Fisler; used by permission. Scripture quotations are from the Holy Bible, New International Version®; copyright 1973, 1978, 1984 by the International Bible Society; used by permission of Zondervan Publishing House.

Printed in the United States of America.

97 98 99 00 01 02 03 04 05 06 / QH / 10 9 8 7 6 5 4 3 2 1 •

Dedication

Ruthann Winans

Writing this book has caused me to reflect on the golden years of my childhood. My parents, Armand and Esther Mattia, and their parents, Felix and Mary Mattia and James and Frances Cannizzaro (known to me as Grandma and Grandpa), have sewn the bright colors of a wonderful Italian heritage into my patchwork quilt of memories. Together with my brothers David and Donny, my sister Sherry, and my aunts, uncles, and cousins, we have shared the simple homespun joys of many family gatherings. Our house was filled with excitement, abundant and delicious foods from the "old country," gospel sing-alongs, and lively conversations round a lace covered table. These are the memories that cause me to look back with heartfelt nostalgia. And so, I dedicate this book to my big Italian family and say, "Grazie! I love you."

Linda Lee

I am profoundly grateful for the rich inheritance given to me by my family. From the Winans, I learned to appreciate leisurely rides down scenic little country roads that led nowhere. From the Coxes, I learned to cherish the satisfying sound of voices joined in sweet harmony. Mom, your caring and nurturing ways continue to be my ideal. Dad, I admire your creativity and ingenuity. Gary, I think I'll always find myself looking up to you. Bruce, your perspective on life is refreshing. Holly, I began to believe in miracles on the day you were born. God put us together as a family, and for that I am truly thankful. I wouldn't have chosen to share this journey of life with anyone but you. It is to you, and all the other good and decent families like you, that I lovingly dedicate this book.

Contents

Patchwork Memories   7

1

Sewing Threads of Love   11

2

Sewing Threads of Value   21

3

Sewing Threads of Delight   31

4

Sewing Threads of Comfort 39

5

Sewing Threads of Tradition 47

6

Sewing Threads of Celebration 57

7

Sewing Threads of Remembrance 69

Patchwork Memories

*B*efore the glowing embers of a fieldstone hearth, a silver–haired grandma is piecing together a homey patchwork quilt. She rocks slowly back and forth as her weathered fingers effortlessly attend to the familiar work before them. In her lap lays a stack of softly faded quilt blocks, prudently cut from clothing once worn by those she holds dear to her heart. Each block is a fond recollection of a moment they've shared—cherished moments that have colored the fabric of their life with laughter and tears, beginnings and endings.

With her tiny needle and a length of sturdy thread, she blesses these ordinary bits and pieces of fabric with the investment of her time. Her steady stitches will bind the quilt securely together, just as love and faithfulness have securely united her family throughout the ever-changing seasons of life.

Under Grandma's loving touch, the hopelessly ordinary is transformed into a priceless treasure—a patchwork quilt of memories—a lasting reminder of the life they've shared together.

Join us on a sentimental journey to Grandma's cottage, a homey place where heirloom quilts and patchwork memories are made. From the stories, reminiscences, and age-old wisdom of this quilter, you will learn to make your own family heirloom quilt. Not a quilt made from blocks of fabric, but a quilt made of memories, precious memories that are just waiting to be discovered in the ordinary moments of life.

Ordinary moments spent chatting after school, making dinner together, or helping with homework—these are the memories your child will truly treasure, simply because they are permeated with the special warmth and love that only you can give.

To take this journey, you must first come to think of yourself as a quilt maker, like Grandma. Begin to see each day of your life as an opportunity for "giving love a memory." Value even the smallest moments as treasured patchwork memories for your quilt, and then bind them together with the steady stitches of your love.

Take as your first inspiration one family who made a charming patchwork memory from something as ordinary as rhubarb! The children have great memories of laughing and playing near the edge of the rhubarb patch all summer long. After the harvest, they worked side by side with their mom and helped her to prepare the regal purple stalks. From those bitter stalks, Mom baked her tasty rhubarb pies. They were a favorite at meals and celebrations the family shared together. And when they were grown and came back for a visit, Mom always made sure she sent them home with a hug and one of her rhubarb pies. To this day, those children think of rhubarb with fond nostalgia, for it came to symbolize the warmth and love they experienced at home.

You, too, can make a delightful memory from something just that ordinary! And the best part is, it's *never* too late to start. Even if your child is an adult with grown children of his own, there is still time . . . time to experience the exquisite joy of ordinary moments . . . time to bless your child with the gift of your love . . . time to make a patchwork memory.

When all is said and done, the most valuable inheritance you will leave your child is the legacy of memories—memories of a home filled with love, timeless values, simple delights, homespun comforts, cherished traditions, joyous celebrations, and fond remembrance. These are the treasures that can never be lost or stolen. They're the most important riches that it will ever be your privilege to pass on.

CHAPTER 1

Sewing Threads of Love

To receive a homemade quilt is to be honored by the ultimate gift . . . love. A single hand-stitched quilt may be more than a year in the making, representing hundreds of hours of work, yards of fabric salvaged from scraps, and thousands of tiny stitches. It's no wonder that quilts came to be regarded as tokens of affection and esteem, for they provide more than welcome warmth on a chilly night. A homemade quilt wraps the heart in the warmth of the quilter's love.

So, too, the threads of our unconditional love bring warmth to the hearts and lives of our children. From the time our wee ones arrive, heaven scented and singing of the miracle of birth, till the day we say our final goodbyes, our children will never lose the fundamental need to know that we absolutely, unconditionally love them.

To a child, unconditional love looks like a homemade cookie, a listening ear, and a comforting smile. To a child, unconditional love feels like a piggyback ride, a bear hug, and a kiss good night. To a child, unconditional love sounds like "I love you," "I'm sorry," "yes," and even the word "no."

By our attitude, actions, and words we convey our message of love—a love that says: *I'm glad you were born, I'm committed to you no matter what, I value you, I believe in you, I like being with you, I'll always love you.* There is security and strength in that kind of love.

Sewing the threads of love costs us nothing, but it is by no means cheap. It's bought with the priceless commodities of our time and energy, resources we often find in short supply. And yet, there can be no more honorable or rewarding way to invest yourself in this life than to give your child the ultimate gift of your love.

And the greatest of these is love.
I Corinthians 13

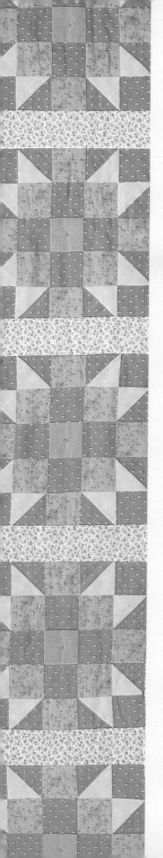

Grandma's Love

Grandma Cox blessed her children with the gift of her homemade patchwork quilts. She delivered them wrapped unassumingly in newsprint and twine, yet her children received them as a priceless treasure nonetheless.

Years later, one of Grandma's quilts was passed on to me. It now occupies a place of honor in my own home. It forever connects my heart to a woman I knew for only the first five years of my life, who still had time enough to leave me with a fond memory of one loving act. Grandma sewed the threads of love in my young life one day when she simply deemed me worthy of drinking from one of her teacups.

To understand the significance of the gesture you must first know that Grandma lived a difficult life, not unlike women before her who forged a life on the American frontier. She became a seasoned homemaker at an early age when, after the death of her father, her mother was forced to work outside the home. Grandma married at the age of 15 and delivered all but one of her nine children at home on their farm. She provided their food from her garden, and she sewed most everything they wore. By necessity, they lived a frugal life where *"Everything was used but the squeal of the pig!"* as Grandma liked to say. They didn't have money for many extras, but twice the few things they did manage to buy were destroyed by tornadoes.

This was the life experience of the woman who gladly handed over one of her few prized possessions to the unsteady hands of a little wide-eyed five year old. She demonstrated her love when she considered me to be worthy of her best. I knew then that she loved me.

A beautiful patchwork memory can be sewn from something as unremarkable as the offering of a cup of tea, when your actions are permeated with love. Let the kindness of everyday life speak the healing words of love to your child's heart. By doing so, day in and day out, you will convey the message your child most wants to hear—that you do indeed love him.

A quilt, made by her own hands, is the only keepsake Grandma was able to leave to me. But to this day it remains one of the most precious things that I own, for it will always remind me of my grandma's love.

Linda

The heart has its own memory, like the mind,
and in it are enshrined the precious keepsakes, into which
is wrought the giver's loving thought.

Henry Wadsworth Longfellow

Chalkboard Chats

A chalkboard in the kitchen is a fun way to communicate love to your family. Write inspiring messages like "Our kids are the best!" or "Way to go, Heather! You won the game!" It's a simple way to affirm your affection for them.

One father uses this same idea and writes his weekly message of love in secret code. He abbreviates each word using just the first letter. The reward for deciphering the code is a date with Dad!

You Are So Special to Me!

Tell your children about the wonderful day they came into your life. Oooh and ahhh over their baby pictures. Let them know how happy you were on their very first birthday!

I often tell my daughter Ashley that when I was young I dreamed of having a red-haired little girl to hold in my arms. Well, lo and behold, many years later it happened. I couldn't believe it when I first laid eyes on her and realized her little head was covered with soft, apricot-colored fuzz. So sometimes out of the blue I'll tell her, "Ashley, *you* are my dream come true!"

13

The Blessing of a Name

How sweet to a child's ears is the sound of his own name. The "name blessing" is a tradition of simply blessing a child by explaining to him the significance and meaning of his name. Children also love hearing the story of how they were named.

As an added blessing, use their name acrostic style with words that describe them: For instance, **JARED** would love to know that: **J** stands for *joyful*, **A** stands for *adorable*, **R** stands for *refreshing*, **E** stands for *esteemed*, and **D** stands for *delightful*. Say or sing it while in the car, at the table, or at bedtime.

Sweet Dreams

Send your child to sleep with sweet dreams. Place a handwritten note on top of their pillow inviting them to join you for a late-night treat of yummy cookies and ice cold milk. If you have more than one child, take turns once a month so each child can look forward to their own special one-on-one time with you. While you snack, ask them to describe what their most fun day would be. Then plan to do one of those fun things.

Sweet Dreams Cookies

This pillowy soft cookie is a comforting nighttime snack. Keep these ingredients handy and you'll always be ready to bake these treats for that special time with your dear one.

1 box yellow cake mix
1/2 stick soft margarine
1/2 cup milk
1 egg
Preheat oven to 350 degrees.

Mix the ingredients into a dough. Spoon walnut-size pieces onto a greased cookie sheet. Bake for 10-11 minutes. (Do not overbake, cookies should not turn brown.) Makes 2 dozen cookies. Cool completely before icing.

Dreamy Icing

Take one can of store-bought vanilla cake frosting. Spoon into a microwave-safe bowl. Heat in the microwave until bubbly. Stir well. While hot, drizzle icing over the cooled cookies. Enjoy a taste of heaven!

*A child's cravings for sweets
is a call of nature. It is necessary
to the proper development of their bodies.*

Laura Ingalls Wilder

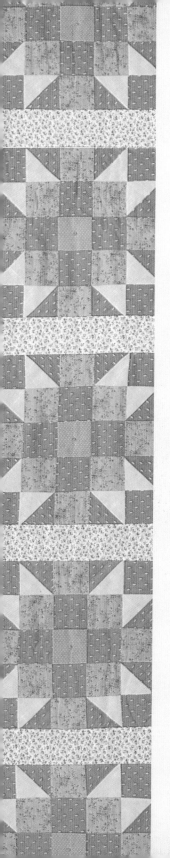

A Pocketful of Love

There is nothing more dear than receiving a note of love and encouragement from those who mean the most to us. Create a "pocket" with a strap attached, to hang on your child's bedroom doorknob or bedpost. (A small basket would work well too.) Then, several times a week, tuck in a message of praise, comfort, appreciation, and if need be, apology. Personalize it as it relates to the things that are happening in your child's life. And every once in a while it would be fun to leave a little treasure that would delight his or her heart—baseball cards, a lollipop, a book, colored markers, or even an invitation to the ice-cream parlor! Your children will learn the value of the written word, and, most importantly, how truly valuable they are to you.

Proud as Punch

Kids feel loved when their parents openly display pride and joy in them. One way to put a gleam in your children's eyes is to hang a sign, near your front door, boldly proclaiming this heartfelt sentiment:

Home of the Greatest Kids on Earth!
Dusty!
Ashley!
J.J.!
(Listing the names of your children)

Use your computer to design this message. Then frame it and hang above your doorbell. Or, if you are a "crafty" person, use paint pens to write this phrase on a strip of painted wood, shaped like a ribbon banner. Add each child's name to an individual wooden heart-shaped cut-out (available at most craft shops). Glue the wood cut-outs to a grapevine wreath trimmed with a bow, and hang on your front door. Each time your child catches a glimpse of this sign a thought will be whispered in his heart, "This is where I belong. This is where I am loved."

Every day of my early elementary school years
I anxiously awaited lunchtime. I would slowly open my lunch box
and peek inside, hoping to find the one thing
that made lunch worthwhile . . . a note from my mom.

Brianne Lee

A Kiss to Keep

Sometimes it's very hard for little ones to be momentarily separated from the comforts of their mother. This can happen at bedtime or when leaving your children in the care of others. One simple and sweet way of comforting them is to imprint a lipstick "kiss of love" in the palm of their hand. This is for them to keep and hold onto, until you return. Tell your child that if the kiss wears off, you have a lot more kisses where that one came from!

Hugging Hands

When you hold the hand of someone you love, it is a hand hug. It's a warm way of saying, "We belong together."

Start a "hand hug" tradition with your children. Try sending a silent message by gently squeezing their hand three times to say "I-LOVE-YOU." Or you can generate a train style "hand hug" when you say grace at the table. After the "amen," the person at the head of the table (the conductor) sends a "hand hug." Pass it from one person to the next, until it has gone all around the table. It's a Hug Train! "All Aboard!"

Patches of Love

*T*ake these little patches of Love, and sew them into your children's lives, and one day their patchwork quilt of memories will be the dearest thing to their heart.

- ❧ Fathers, always remember your daughter's birthday with flowers.
- ❧ Frame your child's artwork and tell her that she is your favorite artist.
- ❧ After grace is said at mealtime, give a hand clap to applaud the cook.
- ❧ Every so often take your child on a special date to spend some one-on-one time with him.
- ❧ Tell your children often, "There is nothing that you could ever do that would make me stop loving you!"
- ❧ Take lots of pictures and show them off.

18

Cherished Moments

Something simple that made me feel loved as a child.

_____

_____

_____

_____

_____

Something simple I do to show my child I love him.

_____

_____

_____

_____

_____

I love these little people; and it is not a slight thing when they,
who are so fresh from God, love us.

Charles Dickens

CHAPTER 2

Sewing Threads of Value

I n the nineteenth century, quilt making was regarded as a valuable skill for women like Sarah. Even as a child, she was expected to diligently practice her needlework. At the age many girls today are just learning to sew, Sarah was already an experienced quilter. By the time she was old enough to marry, she had a full baker's dozen of her handmade quilts in her trousseau. She continued her lifelong dedication to quilt making long into her golden years, working on literally hundreds of quilts over the course of her lifetime. Wouldn't Sarah be surprised to learn that the skill women of her day found so valuable is now more of a novelty among homemakers?

Though time has changed the importance we place on the skill of quilting, the passage of time cannot change the importance of the great underlying values that can be learned from quilters like Sarah. Values like. . .

Patience
Faithfulness
Service

Patience

A good quilter does not make hasty judgments. She thoughtfully sorts through her scraps with a patience born from experience. She redeems what would be trash by seeing her scraps not as they are, but as they could be. As we learn the value of patience, we begin to see ourselves and others through the kind eyes of the quilter.

Faithfulness

A quilt is just a pile of scraps until the quilter commits herself to the job of sewing her patches together. She must remain faithful to the task even though progress is often painstakingly slow. Faithfulness is the value that motivates us to keep our commitments to ourselves and to others, even when it's difficult to do so.

Service

Quilters know the value of service. Working together at a good old-fashioned quilting bee, a team of quilters accomplish in a matter of days what it would have taken one lone quilter many months to finish. They freely give their time in selfless service to one another and gain the blessed reward of friendship.

The values we learn from the quilter have graced the homes of the happiest families since the beginning of time. Sew the threads of these time-honored values in the lives of your children. Make it a point to provide them with opportunities to add patience, faithfulness, and service to their developing character. By doing so, you will be giving your child an enduring foundation on which the happiest of life's memories may be stitched.

Kindness Begins at Home

Kindness is the fruit of a patient heart. It's often hardest to be kind to those we live with every day, and yet it is at home that we first learn the value of kindness. Each week gather your family together to draw names out of a bowl. Plan to do "secret good deeds" for that person. Secretly make his bed, organize shoes in a closet, bring in the newspaper, lay out her robe and slippers just before bedtime. At the end of the week, try to guess who did your secret good deeds. Take time for thank yous and hugs, and then choose new names if you like. If you are consistent with this, your home life will reflect the bright rays of the golden rule. Thinking of others will become second nature, and the memories of everyday life will be sweeter.

Be a Blessing

We will fill the hearts of our children with compassion, and mercy as we ourselves set an example and provide them opportunities to be of service to others. As a family, be a blessing and do kindnesses for loved ones, neighbors, and friends: prepare a meal to deliver to someone who is sick, write a note to someone who is discouraged, or visit an elderly friend who would treasure a smiling face and warm conversation. Present the concept of caring for others by asking your child, "What person could use some cheering up this week?" Then be sure to follow through with your plans and set a date for blessing that person. The memories of these events will echo in the hearts of your children as they continue to reach out to others with tender loving care.

One truly affectionate soul in a family will exert a sweetening and harmonizing influence upon all its members.

Henry Van Dyke

No act of kindness, no matter how small is ever wasted.

Aesop

Sowing Faithfulness

Faithfulness is a commitment to stick to something, even if doing so is inconvenient or hard. Children learn to be faithful in relationships and responsibilities by following the example and guidance of their parents. One simple way to nurture the value of faithfulness in your child is to encourage him to grow a plant from a tiny seed. Decorate a terra cotta pot by sponge painting a lacy pattern on the surface. Then with a paint pen write the word "faithfulness" along the rim and trim it with a raffia bow. Glue the seed packet to the front of the pot to serve as a reminder of what the plant will look like after it has been properly and faithfully cared for. Fill the pot with soil, plant the seed, and give it its first drink of water. Explain to your child that the seed is a living thing, depending on them for nourishment as much as he depends on you. From this teachable moment, and many more like it, a memory will begin to grow; a lesson in faithfulness . . . you reap what you sow.

Lessons learned at mother's knee, last through life.
Laura Ingalls Wilder

Counting on a Promise

Keeping promises is one of the best ways to teach faithfulness, for faithfulness and love go hand in hand. When your child knows he can count on you to keep your word, then your love is evident. "I can always count on Dad to be there at my baseball games" or "I can always count on Mom for her comforting words." These are words spoken from kids with faithful parents.

Make a memory tonight. When you tuck your child into bed, no matter how old he is, take his hand in yours, and gently squeeze each of his fingertips in turn, as you say these words: "I-WILL-ALWAYS-LOVE-YOU!" Tell him this is a promise that he can always count on!

Whistle While You Wait

For our children, having to wait for cookies to finish baking, while their heavenly aroma permeates the air, takes patience. Waiting for Mom to finish her work or her telephone conversation can be extremely difficult. And waiting for the arrival of holidays, birthdays, and summer vacation can be almost unbearable! Patience is easier to come by when we learn to entertain ourselves and keep busy while we wait. Here are some ideas that will help your kids whistle the happy tune of patience:

Mom's Busy Basket

For those times when your child and your work need attention at the same time, have a "Busy Basket" handy to ease the wait for your child. Fill the box with age-appropriate trinkets: old buttons to sort and string, stickers and a sticker book, colorful blocks to stack, clay to shape, etc. Add a kitchen timer so your child can measure the time when you say, "Just ten more minutes." The goodies in this box should be reserved only for those times when "Mom's busy" and given as a reward when your child is exhibiting patience.

5–4–3–2–1– Hurray!

Counting down the days to celebrated events adds to the excitement and fun! The anticipation and preparations can be just as joy-filled as the occasion itself. (It also makes it easier to be patient until that fun day arrives!) Use a small chalkboard to record the number of days until your next celebrated event. It might read like this:

Hurray! Only *17* more days until Grandma and Grandpa arrive!

Decorate the frame to give it a festive look, and hang it in the kitchen to chart the days until happy celebration memories will be made!

The Taste of Patience

Teach your child patience by making butter the old-fashioned way! Fill a small, clean glass jar halfway with whipping cream. Attach the lid tightly. Then put on some music and shake! shake! shake! Keep shaking until the cream thickens. Talk about where the cream comes from and sing "Old MacDonald Had a Farm." Then, before you know it, you've made butter! Stir in a dash of salt, and have some crackers ready to taste the reward of your patience! Read the story of "The Little Red Hen" along with your snack.

Always have a good stock of patience laid by, and be sure you put it where you can easily find it.

The Royal Path of Life, 1881

A Keepsake of Patience

During the early pioneer days, children learned life skills in the art of needlework. As a part of their schooling they spent many hours carefully stitching the alphabet, numbers, and homey quotes. Creating these samplers gave children the opportunity to develop perseverance. The reward was a completed work of art. It was often mounted, framed, and hung in a prominent place in the home for all to see. It served as a reminder of the rewards of patience.

You can give your child the opportunity to create a similar sampler. Put a eight-by-ten inch piece of muslin in an embroidery hoop. Have your child write out this saying with a fine felt tip pen: **Patience, like quilting, is made stitch by stitch.**

(Don't worry if the lines are crooked—it will add to the homemade charm.) Then have your child sew a running stitch over the top of the words. Sew or glue on a few buttons and even some tiny colorful patches of calico. Tea stain it for an antique look and you've got an adorable keepsake to frame and hang in a special spot in your own home!

A Basket of Friendship

In the mid-1800s American women shared Autograph Albums and sewed Friendship Quilts as a way of honoring their neighbors and friends. The work of their hands and the signing of their name brought forth a memorable gift of love. Today, your family can continue this friendly custom by giving away a "Friendship Basket."

With indelible ink, have your family members sign their names in the corner of a large white cotton napkin. Line a basket with the napkin and fill it with homemade goodies: cookies, cocoa mix, a loaf of homemade bread, or even fresh fruit. To add even more old-fashioned charm, tuck in an Autograph Album. Include the names of your family, your address, some words of wisdom, a favorite Scripture, or even a recipe. Tie a bow to the handle where you have attached a laminated card that reads like this:

Friendship Basket

*This basket's filled with goodies
and my best wishes too,
For my life is sweeter because of
friends like you.
Enjoy the things I've tucked inside,
then fill it up anew,
And pass it on to someone else who's
been a friend to you.
May this basket honor friendships whether
they be near or far,
And show those who receive it just how
special that they are!*

Patches of Value

Take these little patches of Value and sew them into your children's lives, and one day their patchwork quilt of memories will be a gentle reminder to be good to others and to themselves.

- Teach your children to find the good in things.
- Encourage teamwork. Praise your children when they work diligently together.
- Give your children three plastic jars—one for saving their money, one for spending, and the other for tithe or charity.
- Invite a family that is new to your area to come to your home for dinner or for the holidays.
- Teach your children the art of letter writing. Provide stationery and stamps. Assign one day a month to write thank you notes and correspondence to loved ones. When your kids are grown and gone, you'll be glad they formed a habit of writing letters!

Cherished Moments

A timeless value I learned from my parents.

_____

_____

_____

_____

_____

_____

Ways I can teach timeless values to my children.

_____

_____

_____

_____

_____

However fleeting and changeable life may appear to be on the surface,
we know that the great underlying values of life are always the same;
no different today than they were a thousand years ago.

Laura Ingalls Wilder

S.T.Sirak 95

CHAPTER 3

Sewing Threads of Delight

Log Cabins, Bear Paws, Turkey Tracks, Honeycomb, a Rocky Road to Kansas, and Broken Dishes are just some of the simple everyday things that have provided inspiration for charming quilt patterns over the years. It's obvious by the pattern names that some of these early quilters had both a vivid imagination and a great sense of humor!

Most of us would be hard put to find inspiration in the modern day counterparts to these quilt patterns. Just try to come up with a whimsical and colorful design that charmingly represents . . . condominiums, poodle paws, pigeon tracks, frozen yogurt, busy highway to Los Angeles, or even broken dishes. But many pioneer women did just that. They experienced a life on the American frontier that was often harsh and desolate and still found sources of delight to inspire them.

Finding delight in simple everyday things has a miraculous way of changing the way we look at our circumstances. (The creator of the Broken Dish pattern must have discovered that!)

Begin your search for the delight by having a good laugh. Make it a family project to find a favorite comic strip, a good book of jokes, or an old family photo album, then allow yourself to laugh until your sides ache. *Do this every day!*

Next, slow down your hurried pace of life and make time for bug catching, flower sniffing, baby rocking, cookie baking, sunset watching, hand holding, and heart-to-heart talking. *Do this every day!*

Finally, find some good in each and every day, then make sure you tell each other about it. There is always something to be thankful for. *Do this every day!*

You'll begin to feel the benefits almost immediately. You won't hold your jaw so tight, and you'll find kind words less difficult to come by. But you'll know for sure that you're on the right track when you notice strangers smiling back at you because, without knowing it, you've been wearing the genuine smile of delight.

Slowly but surely you will find the colorful threads of delight appearing in your family's quilt of memories. And when your children strike out on their own someday, they will bless the lives of everyone they meet with their delightful perspective—a perspective that will serve them well on their journey of life.

A Rainy Day Picnic

There is an old saying, "When life gave Momma scraps, she made quilts!" It's all about making the best of each situation. When unexpected showers cancel a picnic, bring the fun indoors! Light a crackling fire, pop some sweet Kettle Korn, and start your very own "Rainy Day Picnic" tradition! Scoot back the furniture, spread out a picnic blanket, and throw an impromptu picnic indoors. Enjoy a tasty picnic lunch, sing campfire songs, watch an old movie, and swap silly stories. Break a few rules, eat dessert first! It'll become such a favorite, that you'll want to treat yourselves to one even when it's not raining.

Kettle Korn

We first tasted this delicious sugared popcorn in St. Charles, Missouri, and it is a real treat! To make it, add two tablespoons of oil and three tablespoons of granulated sugar to a self-stirring popcorn popper. Add the usual amount of popcorn kernels. Plug it in and pop! It's so finger-licking good, you may want to make two batches!

The Gift of Laughter

Nothing brightens the home like laughter! Begin collecting cartoons from the newspaper (the ones that tickle your funny bone!). Put them on your family bulletin board or refrigerator, for the whole family to enjoy. When it's time to replace the old comics with new ones, start a scrapbook of "Our Family's Funny Memories." Along with the cartoons, add "funny face" photos and journal entries of humorous things that were done or said during family times. The gift of laughter will keep on giving, as each smiling memory is recalled.

Talent Show

Many of us as children developed special talents to amaze or amuse our friends and family: silly noises, impressions, tongue twisters, tricks, or stunts. Don't be afraid to be a kid in front of your kids. Have your own fun-filled family talent show and be remembered by your children in a whole new way!

Treasures to Show and Tell

Make a "Family Treasure Basket" and give it a place of honor in your home. Fill it with little treasures you and your children find—rocks, feathers, an antique pair of spectacles (imagine who wore them!), an old railroad spike, or a twig with lacy green moss. From time to time bring out your basket for show and tell. It's a simple pleasure your kids will treasure.

Treasuring the Little Things

When our children come to discover the wonder of simple pleasures, they will continually experience sweet surprises throughout their entire life. Take a moment every day to point out to your child the scent of a gardenia, the sound of the ocean in a shell, the taste of hot chocolate after coming in from the cold, and the enchantment of fireflies on warm summer evenings. Talk about why those things are special enough to treasure.

My children know that when a sunset has washed the heavens with its brilliant colors of red, purple, orange, and blue, we call for everyone to come and see the beautiful picture God has painted for us in the sky!

The Wonder of Daybreak

At least once in your child's life let him experience the awesome beauty of a summer sunrise. Twenty minutes before dawn, find a place to sit outdoors. Listen quietly and carefully as the earth begins to yawn its "good morning" sounds. With a hushed voice, point out the things you observe. Listen for the first bird chirps and the dog barking in the distance, and watch as the color of daybreak bathes the yard in hues of pink and gold. It doesn't take long for the world to wake up and begin living the day, and yet the memory of these moments will last a lifetime of mornings.

A Happy Dream Box

The words "time for bed" do not usually delight the heart of a child. One way to make bedtime moments a little more enjoyable is to keep a Happy Dream Box at her bedside. Wrap a shoe box in pretty paper and fill it with "happy" pictures cut from magazines: laughing children, animals, toys, food, beautiful outdoor scenes. Each night as you tuck your child in, have her pull out one picture to talk about. Make up a short story together. Then after a prayer, a kiss, and a hug, wish her "happy dreams."

They're Playing Our Song!

Music is a wonderful way to fill our lives with joy, especially when a piece of music is chosen as "Our Song." Songs like "Zippity Do Dah," or "It's A Small World" are fun to sing on long trips in the car or around the supper table. These are great times to cherish musical moments together.

In the Winans' home, after the blessing of the food, we enjoy singing the Johnny Appleseed song "Oh the Lord is good to me . . ." And what could be sweeter than singing a lullaby to our children at bedtime? I sang "Silent Night" at Dusty's bedside, and "Oh How He Loves You and Me" at Ashley's. And for J. J.? Well, as funny as it sounds, I sang the first part of an old Nestle's chocolate television commercial, and he filled in the last word, "Nestle's makes the very best . . . CHOCOLATE!"

35

Heritage of Humor

Family reunions are a wonderful source for humorous stories. My mom has a great story about her grandpa and a raccoon. It seems that Grandpa was having himself a good old mouth hangin' open snooze one day. The sight and the sounds coming from Grandpa's mouth were just too much for their curious pet raccoon to resist. Grandpa woke up to find that raccoon's paw in his mouth. A rambunctious chase ensued, and a great humorous story was added to the Cox family heritage!

Search out humorous family stories and start a collection. Make it a project you do together with the child you love. Videotape, record, or write down the stories as they are told to you, and you'll have a delightful bit of family history to brighten your day whenever needed.

Patches of Delight

Take these little patches of Delight, and sew them into your children's lives, and one day their patchwork quilt of memories will bring a smile to their face and a sparkle to their eyes!

- Play hide-and-go-seek with your kids.
- Put extra marshmallows in their hot chocolate.
- Tape-record your kids singing songs, reading a story, and telling jokes. Play it in the car on long trips.

- Together as a family, gaze at the stars on a clear summer night, and have each person pick out one star to call their very own. The next night see who can be the first to find their star.
- As long as you are able, give your kids piggyback rides.
- Let your kids build forts and tents, both inside and outside of the house.
- Wake up the birthday child with a song and serve him a muffin with a glowing candle on top.

Cherished Moments

Simple delights from my childhood.

_____

_____

_____

_____

_____

_____

One simple delight I'd like my children to experience every day.

_____

_____

_____

_____

_____

_____

A cheerful heart is good medicine.
The Proverbs

CHAPTER 4

Sewing Threads of Comfort

Weary from travel but driven by longing, a young man strides down the stately tree-lined streets of his youth. His heart beats faster and his steps quicken as the scene before him becomes increasingly familiar. It's been far too long since he last savored the comforts of home.

He wonders, "Wouldn't it be something if everything is just as I remember it? Mom's in the kitchen baking apple crumb cake, and Dad's out front tinkering with that old car of his. Billy's shining up the red wagon Grandad gave him, and Boots the cat is peacefully napping on the quilt at the foot of my old bed." Yes. That's the home he's been longing for.

And when they all see him come walking up the path that leads home? Well, he's been thinking about that, too. He knows for certain they'll drop whatever they're doing and come running to embrace the one who has finally returned to them.

He reaches the bend in the road and his heart skips a beat as his eyes finally rest on the long awaited sight of home. He strains to see Mom and Dad, who are now eagerly walking out to greet him. Not far behind, little Billy jumps about wildly, showing his childlike enthusiasm. In the warmth of their tender embrace, the young man breathes a sigh of relief. "I'm home . . . finally home."

The threads of comfort run strong and deep through that place we call home. Far more than a roof over our head, our family home is a place of refuge from the cold world outside. It's a haven of familiarity and belonging, a soothing retreat for body and soul.

A comforting home is a delight to the heart and the senses. Familiar sights, sounds, aromas, and tastes all lend their own unique design to the fabric of our memories of home. Family photos, a soothing lullaby, spiced cider, a crude clay vase made by chubby little fingers: these are the kinds of simple touches that remind us that this is where we belong.

Nurture your child in a home graced with simple touches, and he will soon regard it as a place of abiding comfort. The memories you create there as a family will surely be the dearest and sweetest of all.

Peace and rest at length have come, all the day's long toil is past;
And each heart is whispering, "Home, Home at last!"
Thomas Hood

Comfort Corner

Children and adults alike sometimes need a little time alone—a place to go when they need a quiet time to think or dream or pray. Why not make a comfort corner in your home? Find a secluded corner and tuck a comfy chair into it. A pink lightbulb in a small lamp will give the corner a warm and cozy glow. Then add your own personal touch of comfort with a few of your favorite things:

- a soft quilt or favorite blanket
- a vase of fresh flowers
- a bowl of potpourri
- a basket of favorite books and magazines
- a treasured stuffed animal
- photos of fun times you've shared
- a dish of chocolate kisses

Home Sweet Home in a Box

Familiar objects and reminders of home are just some of the ways you can help a child feel close to you when you have to be separated from him. Make a "Home Sweet Home in a Box" for a child you are going to miss and fill it with some of these comforting goodies:

- a homemade booklet to hold a family picture, a love note, words of wisdom, and a lipstick kiss
- a cassette recording of you reading a favorite story, singing a song, or telling a funny joke
- a handkerchief or soft patch of fabric scented with your cologne
- colorful trinkets and little sweet treats

Where we love is home. Home that our feet may leave, but not our hearts.
Oliver Wendell Holmes

40

The Comforts of Home

When your child is sick (and as a parent you know when it's the real thing), make it a comforting tradition to treat her with some extra tender loving care. Create a comfy bed on the sofa in the family room using fresh sheets and quilts. Arrange fluffy bed pillows and tuck in a hot water bottle for added comfort. Ice chips and crackers, Popsicles and chicken soup are the menu for the day. Add a box of tissue, a favorite video, and R-E-S-T. Though these nurturing tips are just what the doctor ordered to help make the sniffles go away, they are also a welcome treat to lavish on anyone you love.

Storybook Scenes

Every home should have a touch of whimsy to cozy up its corners. Have your children help you create a storybook scene in one of the corners of your house. Use teddy bears, bunnies, or dolls. Give the scene as much detail as you can. For example, to create a tea party theme, set up a doll-size table or lace-covered box with little teacups and tea bags. Add a tiny plate of cookies, napkins cut to size, and a vase of flowers. Then make up a whole

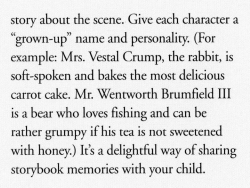

story about the scene. Give each character a "grown-up" name and personality. (For example: Mrs. Vestal Crump, the rabbit, is soft-spoken and bakes the most delicious carrot cake. Mr. Wentworth Brumfield III is a bear who loves fishing and can be rather grumpy if his tea is not sweetened with honey.) It's a delightful way of sharing storybook memories with your child.

My Grandmother's Clock

Talking to our children about their grandparents who live far away can keep the comforting memory of them fresh in their hearts and minds. Watch the national forecast together to see what kind of weather they might be experiencing. Hang a special clock, in a place of honor, set to their time zone. Put a cherished photo next to it. Then imagine aloud what they might be doing at different times of the day: "It's 2:00 P.M. at Grandma's house. She's probably making her apple pie right about now." It will also serve as a comforting reminder that the ones you love so dearly are just a phone call away.

Home is the place where chicken soup makes us well,
a bedtime story puts our children to sleep, and memories keep us warm.
Ruthann Winans

Comfort Food

Every mother should be known for her comfort food—those savory dishes or scrumptious desserts that melt in your mouth.

Whatever it is that your children rave about, make it often. Fill your house with the irresistible aroma of something simmering on the stove. When your kids walk in the door, they'll take a deep breath and think with a sigh, "Something smells good . . . Mom must be home . . . everything's going to be all right!"

Make your house a place
your family wants
to come home to.
Ruthann Winans

Hearty Chicken Noodle Soup

A warm welcome home on a blustery day.
In a soup pot, sauté the following ingredients until the chicken is cooked:
  1 tablespoon olive oil
  2 whole boneless, skinless chicken
  breasts (diced)
  1 large onion (diced)
  3 stalks celery (diced)
  2 cloves garlic (crushed)
  pepper and "Vegit"
  spice to taste

Then add the following ingredients and simmer for 15 to 20 minutes:
  49 ounces chicken broth (canned or homemade)
  1/2 cup fresh parsley (chopped)
  1/4 cup carrot (diced)
Just before serving add:
  1/4 cup peas
  4 ounces cooked and drained
    egg noodles
  Pepper or "Vegit" as needed

When the weather turned blustery and cold outside, Mom always kept a savory pot of her nourishing homemade soup simmering on the back of the stove for us. To this day, there are few things more soothing to my tired body and soul than coming home to the welcoming embrace of her hearty homemade soup.
Linda Lee

Patches of Comfort

*T*ake these little patches of Comfort and sew them into your children's lives, and one day their patchwork quilt of memories will bring them comfort, as they look back and remember that special place called home.

- At bedtime give your child a soothing back rub along with words of encouragement and praise.
- Get in the habit of kissing your children hello and goodbye.
- Set a vase of fresh flowers on your child's nightstand.
- Start a "Walton's Tradition." After everyone is tucked in for the night, call out your good nights to each other.
- Always keep a roll of store-bought refrigerator cookie dough for quick "fresh from the oven" after-school treats.
- Always accompany a consoling hug with "There, there. Everything's going to be all right."
- Always listen with a loving heart.

Cherished Moments

Pleasant things I remember about my childhood home.

_____

_____

_____

_____

_____

_____

Simple ways I'd like to make my home more comforting to my children.

_____

_____

_____

_____

_____

Home, the spot of earth supremely blest,
A dearer, sweeter spot than all the rest.
Robert Montgomery

CHAPTER 5

Sewing Threads of Tradition

On countless moonlit nights, a host of twinkling stars have kept silent vigil over the tender traditions of bedtime. The dark veil of night cannot obscure the windows of home, for they are aglow with fresh scrubbed cherub faces and giggly good night embraces.

Mommy tucks her little angel in bed and pulls the warm quilts right up under her chin. She leans down to place a gentle kiss on her curly-headed one—the faint aroma of fresh baked cookies still with her—she leaves behind the sweet scent of her love.

Daddy quietly reads to the child of his delight, in a voice that's gravelly and deep. By the flickering dance of yellow light, he soothes her with his peaceful bedtime lullaby. With his words he carries her into the peaceful dreams of sleep.

The daily rituals of life provide wonderful opportunities to sew the threads of tradition in the lives of our children. The simple truth is that the little things we do consistently each day often become the endearing memories that our children will look back on with heartfelt nostalgia. These daily rituals will become the nurturing traditions that they most want to pass on to their own children.

Search out those daily acts that you treasure most and begin sewing them into patches of tradition for your family quilt of memories. Give them a place of unhurried honor in your home. Saturate them with your wholehearted joy and love, then watch as they become a tradition your children will always cherish.

But Little Bear didn't say anything, for he had
gone to sleep, warm and safe in Big Bear's arms.
Martin Waddell

Grandpa's Tradition

Going to Sunday dinner at the home of my Grandpa and Grandma Cannizzaro was a tradition that we always looked forward to when I was growing up. We'd arrive to find the house bustling with activity as my aunts, uncles, and their families prepared to gather around Grandma's lace-covered table for one of her delicious meals of spaghetti and meatballs. They were gatherings that left me with fond recollections of family and my rich Italian heritage.

Grandpa and Grandma knew how to create the kinds of traditions that held our tight-knit family together. Grandma's traditions almost always involved food and large quantities of it. But Grandpa had a few traditions of his own. One was a secret that Grandma knew nothing about—a tradition that broke her rule of no sweets before dinner.

Grandpa's tradition was reserved just for his beloved grandchildren, and I loved it. He'd squeeze my little cheeks and in his thick Italian accent he'd say, "I'm-a so glad to see you, my Dolly!" Then he'd whisper, "Grandpa have a surprise for you." Though we played out this scene many times, it never ceased to thrill me when he reached into the pocket of his baggy gray trousers and pulled out a roll of Life-Savers candies from its hiding place.

Grandpa didn't buy the regular Life-Savers variety pack with the lemon-yellow and lime-green flavors that nobody likes anyway. He always carried a whole roll of the cherry-red ones, the ones everyone knows that kids and Grandpas like best!

Cherry flavored Life-Savers became Grandpa's sweet tradition. It was his way of adding his own unique signature to our quilt of memories. And because of that tradition, his grandchildren came to remember him as a loving and dependable man.

Ruthann

Hearts at Home

Home always seems cozier when the whole family gathers for an evening of old-fashioned fun. Establish the tradition of a weekly Family Fun Night. Pop popcorn, put on skits, have a sing-along, play charades or your favorite board games. End the evening with a delicious dessert while enjoying an Old-Time Story Hour. Keep a festive-looking basket filled with good "read aloud" books on a table or near the hearth for an attractive convenience. Before you begin reading, set a quiet mood by dimming overhead lights and lighting the fireplace or candles. Allow young children to do quiet activities, such as coloring or drawing, to keep hands busy while listening. (Keep special supplies reserved just for storytime.) Plan this special evening, just for your family. It will enrich loving relationships, develop a sense of belonging, and create the most heartwarming memories of home.

School Days

Commemorating the first and last day of school is a wonderful tradition your children will look forward to and enjoy. Send them off to school with a happy thought and a smile. Include a note that reassures them of your confidence in them. After school, take them to the park, to the mall, or to get an ice-cream cone. Spend some time chatting about their day and congratulate them for reaching another milestone in growing up.

The Gift of Faith

A wise parent gives their children the gift of a solid foundation of faith on which to build their future. Talk openly with your children about the hope of your faith. Incorporate faith-building traditions into your daily life: join hands and say grace before you eat, attend church services together regularly, spend time with friends who also share your faith. It's a gift that will give meaning to your children's lives and comfort during difficult times.

Teach a child to choose the right path,
and when he is older he will reamin upon it.
The Book of Proverbs

It's Supper Time!

A tradition that is simple and yet so valuable to the preservation of the family is the supper time tradition. Gathering together for the evening meal should be a high priority, especially in our fast-paced lives. Sharing a homecooked meal nourishes our bodies, and sharing encouraging words nourishes our relationships. It's a perfect time for loved ones to connect with one another, catch up on the day's events, and enjoy one another's company. Whether you've planned a simple or elaborate menu, always be sure to season it with plenty of smiles, courtesy, and love. (Angry words and criticism should not be allowed—they are as appetizing as refrigerator mold!)

- Serve a question of the day at your meal: "What is the best thing that happened to you today?"
- Take turns bringing a new and unusual word to the table (one from the dictionary). Have each person try to guess the meaning, then disclose the true definition.
- Fill a basket with one word "subject matters" to discuss: Love, Faith, Nature, Summer, Music, Vacations, Books, etc.

Ya'll Come!

From American farmhouses all across the country comes an old tradition—a call for loved ones to gather. It's the ringing of the dinner bell and a shout, "Ya'll come!" Find a bell that fits your home decor, perhaps a farm-style triangle, a cowbell, or a handheld brass school bell. Keep it handy in the kitchen, and make it a tradition to ring it at meal-time, family meetings, and for all family celebrations! Ring it to commemorate an "A" on a test, braces taken off, a bite of spinach eaten, the last day of school, a Sunday morning wake-up call, a driver's license, an engagement, and potty training! Make it a tradition to seek opportunities to celebrate the precious moments of life.

An Event to Remember

As our children get older and our family grows, the calendar of traditions and events can be a challenge! Set up a family communications center in the heart of your home. Include a calendar, filled in with all your important dates, and a bulletin board to post notices of "upcoming events." For example, here are some things you might want to post:

- ✐ Your Family Fun Night theme— "The theme this week is 'Honesty.' On Saturday night, come prepared with a skit, story, or song about this subject."
- ✐ Birthdays to celebrate.
- ✐ Good news, such as "Company is coming!"
- ✐ A Bible verse to memorize for the week.
- ✐ An inspirational quote.
- ✐ Prayer requests.
- ✐ Love notes and comics to share.
- ✐ The list of chore assignments for the week.
- ✐ Surprise notes, such as a secret invitation to go on a moonlight walk with Dad. These special surprises encourage kids to read and keep current with the family bulletin board.

The Sweet Scent of Comfort

Oftentimes it's the little things we do that give our children a wonderful feeling of warmth and comfort. Little things, such as a pleasing fragrance, can be a comforting reminder of your presence. Each morning smooth on some vanilla-scented hand cream or your favorite cologne. As you hug your children before they leave for school, or when you tuck them into bed at night, your lingering scent will leave them with sweet thoughts of you.

Mom Always Said . . .

There is something comforting about a parent's little words of wisdom—words of love that safely guide a child, in the same way just as a lighthouse helps to keep a ship on course. Find a quote and make it yours. Say it often with love, and someday you may hear the words, "My mom always said . . ."

Little Words of Wisdom

- ✐ "In every situation, ask yourself, what is the right thing to do?"
- ✐ "A day hemmed with prayer is less likely to unravel."
- ✐ "Be kind to unkind people . . . they need it the most."
- ✐ "This too shall pass."
- ✐ "People are more important than things."

What My Family Means to Me . . .

It is usually not until we are grown that we really understand what our family means to us. Yet a parent can begin fostering a love for home and family in the heart of their child at a very young age. Make it a yearly tradition to have each member of the family write down a few thoughts on what their family means to them. Have them also draw and color a family portrait.

Presentation is the key to making this yearly activity a success. Plan an evening filled with fun and food, then gather around the kitchen table set with paper, pens, markers, and a yummy dessert. Don't be surprised, when you share your thoughts and pictures, if you have joyful tears mixed with giggles! Preserve the keepsakes of this special time by putting them in a scrapbook or framing them to hang in your family gallery of happy traditions.

Rise and Shine!

Part of what makes a home happy is the sunny atmosphere we create. Make it a tradition to bring the "sunshine" in every morning as you begin your day. Fill your home with the sound of inspirational music. Bake fresh muffins from the batter you prepared the night before. Ring some jingle bells and go from room to room with a joyful greeting of "rise and shine!" Show your children that you are thankful to have the opportunity to live another day!

Patches of Tradition

Take these little patches of Tradition, and sew them into your children's lives, and one day their patchwork quilt of memories will warm their heart.

- At least once a month cook your child's favorite meal.
- When it's time for the tooth fairy to come, open the window just a crack for her and sprinkle a little Pixie Dust (iridescent glitter) on the sill. And don't let her forget to put a surprise under the pillow!
- A charm bracelet is a lovely tradition for your daughter. Present her with charms to remember vacations, birthdays, holidays, and other rites of passage.

- Read stories to your children while they are taking a bath.
- Go for family walks every night after dinner.
- Have a ten minute snack 'n' chat with your child after school.
- Always greet your children with the words, "Welcome home!"
- Make your well-stocked purse your "signature," what you are known for. Keep inside: gum, candy, a pen and paper, a comb, Tylenol, wet-wipes, tissues, and a Band Aid. (It's comforting to kids to think that their mom can meet most of their needs out of her purse!)

Cherished Moments

A favorite tradition from my childhood.

_____

_____

_____

_____

_____

_____

A tradition I enjoy sharing with my child.

_____

_____

_____

_____

_____

_____

A hundred years from now it will not matter what my bank account was,
the sort of house I lived in, or the kind of car I drove—but the world
may be different because I was important in the life of a child.

Unknown

CHAPTER 6

Sewing Threads of Celebration

The graceful leaf dance of autumn had hardly time enough to take its final bow before Katie was counting the days till Christmas. As the time drew near, Papa decorated their tiny home with lush green boughs of pine, while Mama's kitchen filled the air with the sweet fragrance of gingerbread and taffy. Giddy with anticipation, Katie begged Papa to recite "Twas the Night Before Christmas" each night before she went to bed. And when she was so excited that sleep eluded her, Mama sent her to sleep singing songs of silent nights and winter wonderlands.

When Christmas day finally arrived, Katie was up before dawn. She crept down the staircase and was greeted by the cheery glow of twinkling lights. Festive garlands of popcorn and bright red berries adorned the pine-scented boughs like fine jeweled necklaces. And there from the wrought iron hook on the old oak mantel hung her Christmas stocking. It was stuffed fat with so many shiny oranges and colorful ribbon candies that it looked as if it would surely burst!

But what absolutely delighted Katie's little heart that Christmas laid carefully arranged on the hearth below her stocking. It was a wooden cradle that Papa had made specially for Katie's constant companion, her doll Emma. Mama had lined the cradle with soft flannel and stitched a tiny doll-size quilt that was exactly like the log cabin quilt on Katie's own bed. It was the most wonderful gift Katie had ever received. Indeed, it was a Christmas memory she would treasure for the rest of her life!

The unforgettable memories of celebration have been thrilling the hearts of children since the beginning of time. Steeped in tradition and ceremony, our most beloved celebrations today commemorate the genuine good that is to be found in this life.

By their very nature, our celebrations also serve as important milestones that mark the inevitable passage of time. To a child, a year seems like an eternity. If there were no celebrations to look forward to throughout the year, time would surely stand still for a child. Counting the days until a birthday, Valentine's Day, Easter, Thanksgiving, and—the most grand of all celebrations—Christmas not only brings the sweet joy of anticipation into a child's life, but it provides her with reliable landmarks by which she can judge her own steady progress toward adulthood.

Rekindle the childlike joy of celebration in your heart and home. Relish the traditions and ceremonies that commemorate the genuine good that is to be found in this life. Mark the passage of your child's years with unforgettable memories sewn from the joyful threads of celebration!

Giggles in the Snow

For frosty winter fun, making angels in the snow and building snowmen with your children is a sure way to share lots of giggles and smiles. Celebrating the spontaneous and simple joys of the seasons alongside your child will create memories that will last a lifetime. Kids delight in seeing their parents become childlike and playful. Capture the fun with your camera, and frame the photo along with one of your child's old mittens. Add a short paragraph or poem handwritten by your child describing your time together. Don't forget to have him sign and date it! This will surely become a treasured keepsake and a sentimental conversation starter!

'Tis the season for kindling the fire of hospitality,
the genial fire of charity in the heart.

Washington Irving

Snow Angel Ice Cream

This simple recipe tastes heaven-sent, especially when enjoyed by a warm fire! Keep these ingredients on hand, and you will be ready to celebrate winter's first snowfall with this delicious treat!

2 eggs (pasteurized egg substitute may be used)
1 can sweetened condensed milk
1 teaspoon vanilla
Dash of salt
Large bowl of fresh snow

Beat together the first four ingredients. Add to the snow gradually to prevent lumps. Serve right away. For added flavor, you can drizzle blueberry, maple, or strawberry syrup on top.

*Chill December brings the
sleet, blazing fire and
Christmas treat.*
Mother Goose

Stockings Hung with Care

Hanging stockings from the mantel and filling them with sweet treats and trinkets is a tradition most families enjoy. But sweeter still is a tree adorned with the same tiny socks that kept your baby's tender toes warm. (Colorful winter mittens would also be charming too!) Stuff them with a few cotton balls or fiberfill and tie with a satin ribbon. Remembering the infancy of our dimpled darlings will warm our hearts with a gentle joy as we take a peek backward in time.

Another idea is to help your children decorate their own "stocking" tree, filling the branches with blossoms of Baby's Breath, ribbons, and bows. Tuck in a few of their infant toys and baby pictures that you have backed with sturdy paper and trimmed with rick-rack or tiny buttons. This is a wonderful time to talk about the day your child was born and the first time you held him in your arms. You can also share the story of another special baby whose birthday is on Christmas day—baby Jesus!

Aglow with Holiday Warmth

The soft glow of a Christmas candle, with its halo of bright gold, is a friendly beacon in the window to all who pass by. It reflects a warm and inviting message that says, "Welcome!" Decorating with candles is an early American Christmas tradition that will fill your home with dancing light and cozy charm.

Sleep in Heavenly Peace

What sweeter way to send a child off to dreamland than with their very own special Christmas pillowcase? Using fabric paints, decorate a plain red, blue or green pillowcase with snowmen, pine trees, lollipops, angels, and candy canes. To make it extra special, add your own tender sentiments of love and goodnight blessings. Your loving words will echo in their heart all night long. This same idea would also bless the birthday child as well!

Ideas That Shine

- For a memorable centerpiece set white votives in a shallow crystal bowl of sparkling sugar or rock salt, creating a whimsical scene of "candles in the snow."
- When it's time to step out into the frosty night air for a neighborhood caroling party, provide everyone with a lit tea-candle in a jar. (Fill each jar with two inches of salt to secure the candle.) It will light your pathway and keep your hands toasty warm.
- To delight children and adults alike, put a small candle at each place setting. Then as each person takes a turn to light their candle, have them share a sentiment of what Christmas means to them. When all the candles are lit, and the room is aglow, join hands and softly sing a chorus of "Oh Little Town of Bethlehem." These are the memories that will shine as bright as the Bethlehem star on that first Christmas night.

The most vivid memories of Christmases past are usually not of gifts given or received, but of the spirit of love, the special warmth of Christmas worship, the cherished little habits of the home.

Lois Rand

Bringing the Harvest Home

Picking apples on crisp autumn afternoons is a delightful harvest-time family tradition. Bring a simple picnic lunch to enjoy near the orchard. Tuck in a soft quilt for comfort, a picture book of Johnny Appleseed to share, and a camera for those "memories in the making" moments.

As an alternative, if an apple orchard is not in your area, a drive in the country to visit a farmer's market can be an adventurous treasure hunt as you discover nature's autumn bounty. Take home a basket full of pomegranates, pumpkins, Indian corn, and juicy red apples. Then in celebration of the beauty of fall, adorn the nooks and crannies of your house with these colorful harvest blessings.

Warming the Autumn Chill

Throughout the golden days of fall, keep a steaming kettle or crockpot filled with spicy apple cider. The aroma of this tangy goodness will ribbon its way through the rooms of your home, drawing loved ones to gather and to settle in, as winter whispers a frosty hint of its arrival.

Candy Apple Cider

1 gallon apple cider
1/2 cup brown sugar
8 whole cloves (in tea strainer)
1/2 cup Cinnamon Red
   Hot candies
1 orange (sliced)

Combine ingredients and simmer at medium heat until steaming. Then remove cloves. Turn to medium low heat and cover to keep hot.

Autumn . . . the year's last, loveliest smile.
Bryant

Deck the Halls with Apple Garlands!

The little things we do to create a cozy atmosphere become a delight to the heart and senses. One sure way to add a charming touch to your window, shelf, or mantel is to swag a garland of spicy scented dried apples on them.

To prepare the apples, cut slices crossways (cutting each slice through the core) and soak in lemon juice. Blend a mixture of cinnamon, allspice, ground cloves, and salt. Dip both sides of the apple slices in spice mixture. Dry in oven at 150 to 200 degrees for 6 hours. String on fishing line with the core-side showing (two hole button style). You can also add cinnamon sticks, popped corn, cranberries, and kumquats. Tie raffia bows to finish off the knotted ends.

Mom's Old–Fashioned Apple Crisp

Delight your child with the delicious experience of making this old-time recipe. As you cook side by side, the autumn memories you breathe in will be delicious and joy filled.

Mix together and arrange in a 13 x 9 baking pan:

6 cups peeled and sliced tart apples

3/4 cup sugar

1 teaspoon cinnamon

1/4 cup water

1 teaspoon vanilla (added to water)

Mix topping until crumbly and sprinkle over the apple mixture:

1 cup flour

1 cup oatmeal

1 cup brown sugar

1/8 teaspoon salt

1/2 cup melted butter

1/4 cup chopped pecans (optional)

Bake at 350 degrees for 30-35 minutes or until apples are tender and topping is golden brown. For an added treat, serve warm with vanilla ice cream. Make this a yearly fall tradition!

Counting Our Blessings

The traditional harvest meal shared around a table with family and friends tastes best when served with a generous portion of thankfulness. Beginning the first week of November, decorate a jar or basket and label it, "Our Many Blessings." Pair it with a note pad and pen. Then throughout the month each family member can participate by writing down the things they are thankful for. Put these slips of paper in the basket and wait to read them on Thanksgiving Day. This simple yet gracious tradition will be long remembered and will fill each person with a heartfelt sense of gratefulness.

When you think about your life, don't look at what is missing, be thankful for what is there.

A Holocaust Survivor

Our Family Celebration Tree

Decorating for the seasons brings such joy and delight to the hearts of our children. Keeping a small artificial pine tree or branch (secured in a container filled with plaster of paris) can become a celebration tree for all seasons. For Valentine's Day, adorn the tree with homemade hearts. At Easter, hang colorful eggs and springtime flowers. Add miniature flags for the Fourth of July, and tuck autumn leaves under tiny pumpkins for fall. The tree will only take up a small space in your home, but the memories made will be big enough to fill your whole heart!

65

Patches of Celebration

Take these little patches of Celebration, and sew them into your children's lives, and one day their patchwork quilt of memories will be bright with holiday cheer.

- When your adult child returns home for a visit, put an electric candle in her old bedroom window to celebrate her arrival.
- For an adopted child, celebrate his "Homecoming Day" each year. Honor that wonderful day when you got to bring him home! Bake a cake, give a gift, and stroll through his photo album recalling the story of that blessed day.
- Throughout the holiday season, bring a basket of each day's Christmas cards to the supper table. Read them aloud and enjoy the thoughts of affection from loved ones near and far.

- Start a new advent tradition—celebrate the journey to Bethlehem. Set up an unbreakable manger scene. Place Mary and Joseph in one room and the kings in another. Each day have your child move them closer and closer to the manger scene. Then on Christmas Eve, have them finally arrive in "Bethlehem." Christmas morning, place Baby Jesus in the manger and sing happy birthday to Him!

We do not remember days; we remember moments.
Cesare Pavese

Cherished Moments

My most memorable childhood celebration.

_____

_____

_____

_____

_____

_____

Ways I make celebrations memorable for my children.

_____

_____

_____

_____

_____

_____

Such magic there is in Christmas. . . . Our hearts grow tender with childhood memories
and love of kindred, and we are better throughout the year for
having, in spirit, become a child again at Christmas time.
Laura Ingalls Wilder

CHAPTER 7

Sewing Threads of Remembrance

S moothing out her quilt on the kitchen table before her, Grandma finally lays her needle and thread to rest. Her patchwork quilt is done. She pours herself a good cup of hot coffee, and then settles back in her rocking chair to reminisce a bit. She picks up the old Bible that has been in her family for generations. From its brittle yellow pages, she reads the inscription penned by her great-great-grandmother. It's a line from Ecclesiastes.

To every thing there is a season,
and a time to every purpose under heaven.

During those years when the cottage was filled with the joyful exuberance of children, it had seemed to Grandma that the seasons of her life would never change. "How quiet this old house seems to me now," she chuckles to herself.

She smiles with pride as she gently strokes the colorful patches of her quilt. It's true, the time for raising her children is past. Her babies have babies of their own now. But, those patches on her quilt bring back the blessed memories of their childhood as if they happened just yesterday. "Why, that blue patch came from the dress Mary wore the day she sung her first solo. The yellow check is from a shirt my mama made for baby Thomas. And Bess was wearing the green calico when she graduated as valedictorian of her class." Each patch brings back a flood of memories.

With a cheerful whistle, Grandpa enters the kitchen, his feet all caked with mud from the garden. Grandma quickly brushes away a tear and playfully chides him, "Wipe your feet, Pa!" Grandpa gives her a hug and a warm kiss on the fore-head. Then he notices the meaningful look in her eyes. He runs his rough old hands over the quilt she now holds in her arms and whispers, "We've had a good life, haven't we, Ma?"

"It's been a mighty good life," she thoughtfully agrees. Then looking to the grandfather clock in the corner, she quickly stands to her feet. "Oh dear, where has the day gone? There's no time to waste. Those grandkids of ours will be here any minute."

In no time at all, the little cottage is alive with the laughter of children. Grandma and Grandpa stand, hand in hand, in the middle of the happy bedlam. Their little cottage is quiet no more. They look at those precious grandchildren and they smile—the knowing smile of all those who have seen the seasons of life come and go.

Like Grandma and Grandpa, we, too, will only have our children home for a season. In due time, these sweet moments that we now share with them will one day come to an end. The only thing that will remain from this season of life will be our keepsakes and the treasured memories that they help us to recall.

Commit yourself now to the important task of collecting mementos of your life together—keepsakes that will one day be as precious to you as the patches in Grandma's quilt. Tuck away photos, letters, drawings, handmade gifts, video and tape recordings, anything that will remind you of the patchwork memories that you are making as a family. For through these mementos, you will someday be able to recapture fond memories that would be lost forever without them.

Help your children to develop an interest in preserving their own history, too. Children naturally love to collect things. Give them a special place where they can begin saving what is meaningful to them. Have them tell you the story of their favorite memories. Nurture the sentimental heart of the quilter in your children and someday you will all have a bountiful supply of beautiful memories to share.

The exquisite joy of making and preserving patchwork memories with your children is one of the privileges of this season in your life. It is a unique opportunity that cannot be put off to a more convenient time, for it comes only once.

So today, as you cherish the children you've been blessed with, take a moment to sew the threads of remembrance. Open your eyes and your heart, and try to capture this moment. Relish those dirty fingerprints, crude crayon drawings, and storybooks left on the floor. Savor their rosy little cheeks, soft wet kisses, and big smiling eyes. Paint in your memory a lasting picture of your children just as they are, today. Then, make it a point to tuck away a keepsake to help you remember.

And one day, when *your* home is surprisingly quiet, these keepsakes will bring back sweet memories of this very special season in your life. Your sentimental tokens of remembrance will bring back the warmth and tenderness of the beautiful moments you've shared with your children. Moments just like today.

How dear to this heart are the scenes of my childhood,
when fond recollection recalls them to view; the orchard,
the meadow, the deep-tangled wildwood, and
every loved spot which my infancy knew.

Samuel Woodworth

Cookbook Memories

Cooking a favorite meal is a part of what makes home a special and comforting place. Each time you pull out your cookbook to try a new recipe, or to fix an old standard, make a notation in the margin. Write the date, occasion, and whose favorite it was. Add any other tidbits of trivia. And when your children are grown and begin to search for their favorite recipe, your "Cookbook Memories" will take them back in time on a sentimental journey to that very special place of their childhood.

Keepsake Journal

Little notes with scribbled words given to us by our children are wonderful keepsakes to treasure. But how much more special to begin sharing a journal in which you take turns writing your observations. In a fabric–covered blank book, enter bits and pieces of your daily life, thoughts about the future, questions, and messages of love. In the end, you'll have a wonderful keepsake, a treasure that is valuable beyond words.

Our Family Treasure Wreath

Thinking of our loved ones warms us like a loving embrace. And what more endearing way to reflect on these precious family ties than in our cherished family photographs.

Adorn a wreath or garland of fragrant pine or grapevine with golden framed photos trimmed with ribbon, and it will look like priceless jewels affectionately nestled close together where they belong. Add tiny white lights for an extra sparkle. Duplicates of valuable photographs can be obtained inexpensively by having color copies made of them at a local quick print shop. Be sure to record identifying information on the back such as names, dates, relationships, and events. Share with your children the stories behind the faces.

These pictorial ornaments of our heritage will give our children an enduring sense of belonging and strengthen their own memories of the family tree.

Our family is our treasure.
Heather Lee

Capturing a Moment in Time

What is sweeter than the tender little pink fingers and toes of your child? There is a simple yet endearing way to preserve the memory of their tiny hands and feet. Use a copy machine to capture the image. Then, cut it out and paste it into a baby book, frame it along with their photo to keep or give as a gift, or use it to decorate note cards and stationery.

Treasures for All to See

Keeping the little tokens of our children's growing up days gives them a sense of belonging and a sense of who they are. It also serves as a gentle reminder to us parents that they are growing up and that the time spent with them should be cherished. Bring out of hiding those darling keepsakes of childhood and create a display of treasures to enjoy all the time. Use a china or curio cabinet, or even a shelf or mantel, to display pictures, booties, baby toys, and a tiny outfit to honor the children in your life. They will feel honored and you will have a precious reminder to "cherish the moment."

"My Dear Child . . ."

Begin a new sentimental birthday tradition. Each year write a letter to your child that is to be opened when he becomes an adult. Include a photo and an account of a special moment you have shared, an interesting event in history, or the "fad" of the year. It's a wonderful way to document your involvement in his life and to give him a treasured memoir of your love.

Use a variation of this idea as a special way to communicate with an adult child. Give the child a pretty notebook or large decorated envelope. Then, each month, send her a letter that contains a special memory of a time you've shared, a bit of family history, or a character trait you admire in that child. She'll end up with a delightful collection of your loving thoughts toward her. It's never too late to create an heirloom of remembrance.

Hand-Me-Down Heirloom

Begin today to think about the kinds of things that will someday be your child's treasured heirlooms; Dad's cozy warm flannel shirt, Mom's homemade cross-stitch sampler, Grandma Ruth's secret recipe for yummy chocolate chip cookies, Grandpa Loran's list of fun things to do for $5 or less. Start a special box for each child in which you set aside meaningful keepsakes from your life together. Then hand them down to your children when they have their own home.

I began having "grown up" tea parties with my daughter Ashley when she was four years old. I purchased a pink floral musical teapot and two matching cups, just for our special time together. Now, Ashley is almost thirteen, and this teapot is full of memories. Someday when she has a home of her own, I'll give her this teapot and one of the matching cups. She'll have a treasured heirloom and memories of Mom, and my cup will be overflowing with sweet remembrances of her.

Grandma's Button Jar

There are many treasures in Grandma's house, but her button jar is a favorite! A button jar filled with a multiplicity of colors, shapes, and sizes is always fascinating to a child: buttons from Grandpa's overalls, Mom's wedding gown, Grandma's pink coat. Like the patches on a quilt, each button has a story to tell.

Collect old buttons from the people you love and use them to create whimsical heirlooms to remember them by. Glue them around a frame, then tuck in a favorite photo. String them on embroidery floss and make a necklace or garland. Cluster them together and make an ornament or a special pin to wear when you are feeling extra sentimental. Something as simple as a button can become a lovely and treasured remembrance of those you hold dear.

Grandma's Button Cookies

Whip up a batch of your favorite sugar cookie dough. Roll dough and cut out with a round cookie cutter. Bake as usual. While the cookies are still hot on the cookie sheet, take a drinking straw and poke two or four holes in the middle of each cookie to resemble a button. With tube icing make a crisscross "stitch" between the holes to look like thread. Store them in a jar, top the lid with calico, and label it "Grandma's Button Cookies."

A Treasured Remembrance

Create a Treasured Remembrance. Gather together a vintage photo of a loved one, a patch of fabric from their clothing, buttons, lace, old costume jewelry, and a note or recipe handwritten by the person in the photo. Arrange these keepsakes and glue them to a backing of wallpaper covered cardboard.

Use fabric paint to draw "stitches" around the edge of the patches to give it a hand sewn look. Place the collage in a wood frame. With a paint pen write this sentiment all the way around the entire face of the frame (top, sides, and bottom): "HAPPY MEMORIES OF MY SPECIAL *GRANDMA!*" Embellish the corners of the frame with buttons or charms, and hang this treasured remembrance among your favorite things.

It is threads, hundreds of tiny threads which sew people together through the years.

Simone Signoret

Patches of Remembrance

Take these little patches of Remembrance, and sew them into your children's lives, and they will have cherished memories to pass down to future generations.

- Begin now to save scraps of your family's clothing to have a quilt made from in the future. Using a template, cut them into squares. Store them in sealed plastic bags until you have enough blocks for a quilt along with a note to record bits of trivia such as who wore them, dates, and events. (If you don't sew, contact a local quilt maker in your area.)

- When you give your child a new book, always inscribe it with the date and a personal message of love.

- Tell your children the stories behind your heirlooms, furniture, jewelry, and photographs.

- Take pictures and videos of your child's bedroom (messy and clean!) and other rooms of the house. Someday he will treasure these photos of his childhood home!

- Have your child's grandparents write down their favorite Bible verses, recipes, and words of advice. Save these and give them to your child when he grows up.

Cherished Moments

A keepsake that I treasure.

_____

_____

_____

_____

_____

_____

A sentimental token of rememberance that I'd like to give to my child someday.

_____

_____

_____

_____

_____

_____

*Memories hide in every corner of my house, and I take great
delight every time I stumble across one.*
Unknown